# Build Generational Wealth

## Retire Early

Michael Dillard

Michael A Dillard Publishing

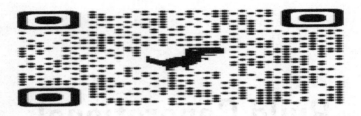

Copyright © 2022 by Michael A Dillard Publishing

www.madillard.com

info@madillard.com

ISBN 978-1-7377828-3-4 print
ISBN 978-1-7377828-2-7 ebook

# Contents

# Chapter One
# INTRODUCTION

*Are you ready to build generational wealth in 5 easy to follow steps? Do you want to know when you can retire? Do you want to know how much money you need to retire?*

A question that I ask most people is, what are you doing for your retirement? Most will say that they have a 401K account with their employer. If you already have a 401K account, then this is GREAT. The next question that I ask people is, what is your employer investing your money in? Everyone will say, "they do not know". Well, as the old saying goes, what you do not know will hurt you. After reading this book, you will have the skills to identify which financial investments are available to help you retire early. You will also learn how easy it is to get out of debt and, most notably, how to build generational wealth.

Why do people spend 70% of their time at work? Why are you getting up 250 days out of 365 days in a year to go to work? When do you plan to stop going to work so that you can enjoy your hard-earned MONEY? Is the money that is in your bank account at this very moment enough to allow you to retire today? Will you be forced to work until age 80 to pay your bills? Do you want to leave an inheritance for your loved ones? After reading this book, you will learn the secrets to building generational wealth in 5 easy to follow steps.

Unlike most books, the five easy-to-follow steps to building generational wealth are taught through people whose lives mirror our own. Marcus and La Toya start their marriage by racking up debt to pay for their wedding. Would it shock you that most marriages end in divorce due to financial problems? This cannot happen to Marcus and La Toya because we need them to stay together so that they can build generational wealth for their family.

What is a 401K? What is a stock or a bond? What is an IRA, and why are they so important?

By now, you are saying, Help, Help, this is getting complicated or thinking to yourself, I thought the five simple steps would be easy. Do not worry, my friend; once you see the five simple steps used by actual people like Marcus and La Toya and other people you can relate to, you will see just how simple the five steps will help you build generational wealth.

There are several ways to reach retirement, just like there are several ways to travel from Tennessee to Florida. You can take the bus and get there in 18 hours, you can drive and get there in 10 hours, or you can fly and get there in 2 hours. This is the same with retirement, you can reach your retirement destination, but the financial tools you select will determine how fast you get to retirement paradise.

# Chapter Two

# WEDDING DEBT

La Toya and Marcus kept running into each other at Mt. Zion Baptist church. One day after the church ended, Marcus invited La Toya to a Tennessee Titans football game day. From that day on, they have been spending quality time together. After two years of dating, the time had finally come for La Toya and Marcus to get married. They sent out wedding invitations to their friends, family, and coworkers three months before the wedding. Yet a few last-minute reservations came the week of the wedding, which put the seating arrangements all out of order. With 24 hours left before the wedding, there were a lot of errands and tasks that needed to be completed. The church decorations were half put up, and the food and beverage menu needed to be finalized due to an issue with the caterer. The costs for the wedding were adding up by the minute.

Marcus was standing in line at Target to buy a few last-minute items for the wedding reception, hoping that this would be his last purchase before saying, "I do." Marcus was incredibly nervous as he walked up to the cashier; he avoided making eye contact with the cashier and slowly placed the items from his shopping cart onto the conveyor belt. Marcus was not sure if his credit card would be declined or not because he had spent more than he had anticipated on the credit card. The only reason Marcus even had a credit card was to use it for points so that he could earn free hotel points. Marcus planned to pay the balance that was on the credit card off every month to earn frequent flyer points and avoid paying 24% APR interest. To pay for the rising wedding costs, Marcus applied for a 2nd credit card online. Before Marcus knew it, he had reached his credit card limit within five days of receiving the credit card in the mail. Marcus found himself buying more and more things for the wedding with no end in sight. La Toya wanted an extravagant wedding, so he could not disappoint her. The cashier hit the total button, and the screen showed $341.21. Marcus slowly handed his credit card to the cashier. He closed his eyes as the cashier hit the process transaction button on the cash register. At first, nothing happened, and then seconds later, the screen flashed, and then the cash register started to make a noise as the receipt began printing out. Woo, Marcus sighed; he was hours away from putting the credit card away. Marcus's uncle Walter and Aunt Ann had agreed to pay for an all-inclusive honeymoon for Marcus and La Toya. Marcus was motivated to get married, say goodbye at the reception and jump on the plane so that they could stop spending money that they did not have.

La Toya wanted the reception to be the talk of the town. She took out a $10,000 loan with a finance company to ensure that the wedding decorations were full of fresh flowers, ribbons, and lots of table decorations. La Toya wanted this moment to be the finest experience ever. She really wanted to go all out so that she could post her pictures all over social media.

Her college friends Renae and Karen were in town to celebrate her special moment book.ren decided to live in Nashville, Tennessee, after graduating from Middle Tennessee State University's

(MTSU) nursing program. Karen has been married to her husband, Chris, a store manager, for three years. Karen works at Vanderbilt Hospital as a pediatric nurse. Renae is from Nashville, Tennessee, and made it her goal to not go into a lot of debt pursuing a college degree. Renae completed two years of liberal arts studies at Nashville State Technical College because the tuition was cheaper, which allowed her to earn an associate degree debt-free. Afterward, Renae transferred to MTSU without applying for a student loan. La Toya, Renae, and Karen were study group friends for accounting 202, and they have been friends ever since. Renae graduated from MTSU with a degree in accounting and now works at Dollar General's corporate office. La Toya completed her studies in Management and worked for an HCA hospital. Marcus's best friend Juan from High School flew in with his wife, Lisa, all the way from Frankfurt, Germany. Juan is an E6 in the U.S Army, and Lisa works at the military base as an HR specialist.

# Chapter Three

# MARCUS' FATHER PASSES AWAY

M arcus' father was the breadwinner of his family. He was a huge promoter of doing whatever it takes to get a college degree so that Marcus did not have to suffer as he did. Marcus's father had been laid off so many times that he lost count, so he promised Marcus that he would pay for his college tuition. However, when Marcus's father passed away unexpectedly, he did not have the money to pay for his college classes, so he dropped out. Marcus's mother had to sell the house because they had just refinanced the home to take cash out to remodel the kitchen and pay for part of Marcus's tuition. His mother could not afford the newly refinanced mortgage payment on her minimum wage salary. Life had taken a turn for the worse for Marcus at the worst moment in time.

Marcus's Uncle Walter has always been there for him after the passing of his father. Marcus really respected his uncle. Every time Uncle Walter spoke, Marcus perked up and focused on every word that he said so that he could catch a jewel of wisdom that his uncle would drop from time to time. When Marcus's Uncle found out that Marcus had dropped out of college, he offered to pay Marcus's tuition for him. Marcus had never thought about asking his uncle for money because he was retired for about five years. He always told Marcus not to spend all his money on things that did not go up in value. Marcus always wondered what happened to his uncle that made him talk about money every time they visited each other. He figured that his uncle did not have much money because he wasted it buying new cars. With the financial help from his uncle, Marcus went on to receive a B.S. in Marketing from Austin Peay State University. After five months of searching for a job, he received a job offer from the State of Tennessee to work as a communication specialist. He packed his bags and moved to Nashville, Tennessee.

La Toya decided to get picked up from her mom and Dad's house instead of her apartment to symbolize the tradition of moving from your parents' house to forming your own husband and wife union. That morning, La Toya was so nervous that she did not want to eat anything. Her emotions were all over the place. At one moment, La Toya felt joyful, then jittery, nervous, and back to upbeat again. Her mother insisted that she should sip on some tea and eat a few crackers so that she did not pass out in front of everyone at the altar. The time had finally come; Marcus and La Toya were about to be happily married.

The church was fully decked out just as La Toya had planned it. The purple, white, and gold décor blended right into the church's allure. It was happening; the bride's maid and best men had just finished walking down the aisle. The bride's maid dresses were beaded and laced in purple lace, which matched the bows in their hair. Everyone was seated quietly and looking back as the pianist played the song "here comes the bride was being played by the pianist." La Toya and her father began their walk down the aisle. La Toya looked just like a princess. Her tiara was sparkling, and her dress fit her like a glove. The train from her dress flowed effortlessly along the aisle as she took one step at a time until she and her father reached Marcus's outstretched hand. La Toya's father and Marcus nodded at one another. Then, her father gently placed La Toya's hand into Marcus's hand.

Marcus had been waiting for this moment ever since their first date at the Tennessee Titans game. He had written a special vow to signify his ever-lasting love for La Toya. The audience gasped with Aww when he read the final word from his vow. La Toya's heart began to beat faster and faster. She was so afraid that she would forget her vows since everything was happening so fast. She took a deep breath and began reading her vows. As she finished, Marcus smiled with joy. The Paster shouted, "you may now kiss the bride!" Marcus gently pulled up La Toya's veil and gave her a slow kiss on the lips. They did it. They were a married couple, joined at the hip. Marcus and La Toya held hands and strolled up the aisle and into the courtyard to take some wedding pictures. Soon the wedding party joined them in the yard to take some pictures together. Then their family and friends joined them to commemorate the special moment.

# Chapter Four

# THE HONEYMOON

Marcus and La Toya had a flight to catch that evening, so they decided to have the wedding reception immediately after the wedding ceremony. They took 20 minutes to collect themselves in a private room, and then they walked hand in hand into the reception hall.

When they walked into the reception hall, everyone was already seated. The live band was on point. You could feel the love in the Air. Chef Reggie's from the Palace of Organic Foods restaurant catered the food.

As soon as Marcus and La Toya were seated, the band paused. The best man stood up and said, raise your glass and let us toast to prosperity, good health, and eternal happiness. The time had come for Marcus and La Toya to rush home, change clothes, grab their bags and drive to the airport. Marcus's uncle insisted on taking them to the Nashville International Airport. As they got out of the car, his uncle handed them a book called "Build Generational Wealth". Marcus tucked the book inside his backpack and thanked him. La Toya and Marcus headed to the check-in counter at the airport. The gate agent congratulated them on just getting married. Their uncle had bought them business class tickets to Cape Town, South Africa, which they were excited about since they had never flown out of the country. After passing through the airport security stations, they walked into the business lounge and sat down. They smiled at each other and held hands. Later, La Toya leaned over into Marcus's arms.

Shortly after that, the lounge attendant walked up to them to inform them that their flight was boarding. Up, up and away, it was the first time that Marcus and La Toya had flown out of the United States of America. They landed in Johannesburg, South Africa, and a private tour guide picked them up and drove them to their bush resort. They checked in, and the receptionist told them that the morning safari starts at 5 am and that they should be on time. They checked into the room and were taken aback by how luxurious it was. There were rose petals on the bed arranged in a heart shape. There was a tray of fruit and milk chocolate on the counter. Shortly after that, there was a knock at the door. The hotel staff had brought them a gift basket which was. a pleasant surprise. They thanked the staff member for the gift and freshened up before heading downstairs for dinner.

After dinner, they went back to the room and crashed since they were extremely exhausted from all the traveling. Marcus and La Toya awoke to the alarm clock's ringing. It was still dark outside as they gathered their attire for their much-anticipated sun-rise safari. The trip was more than worth the 18 hours of flying. They saw elephants, lions, monkeys, zebras, and giraffes for two days straight. It was such a memorable moment. On day three, they flew into Cape Town and stayed in at a bed and breakfast resort along the beach. They could hear the waves crashing against the seashore from their bedroom. They bought tickets for the red bus tour around the city. They hopped on and off the bus, making sure to enjoy all that Cape Town had to offer. The next day they decided to sleep in to rest up for their trip back to

Murfreesboro, Tennessee. Marcus remembered the book that his uncle had handed him at the airport, so he searched through his backpack so that he could start reading the book.

Marcus was amazed at the depth of information written in the book. The book was written in an easy-to-understand language that he could fully understand and comprehend the personal financial advice. He told La Toya about what he had just learned in the book, and she was eager to implement the five steps that the book had taught them. Marcus and La Toya had a new mindset about money. They decided that they wanted to retire early as Marcus's uncle did, and most importantly, they wanted to build generational wealth for their children's children.

# Chapter Five

# 5 STEPS TO BUILD GENERATIONAL WEALTH

*The generational wealth plan was simple:*

**1)** *Buy term life insurance.*
**2)** *Get the free 401K/TSP company match.*
**3)** *Pay off your credit cards and consumer debt.*
**4)** *Put money in an IRA.*
**5)** *Open custodial accounts for your children.*

# Chapter Six

# STEP 1 – BUY LIFE INSURANCE

Soon they were back on the plane flying back home. Marcus' uncle picked them up from the airport and welcomed them back. Marcus was so on fire to start building generational wealth that he called his insurance broker the moment that they arrived back from their honeymoon and asked to purchase 25 years of term life insurance in the amount of $875,000 for himself and $1,125,000 for La Toya. Since Marcus's salary was $35,000 a year, he multiplied his salary times 25 years, totaling $875,000. Marcus wanted to make sure that if something happened to him, his children would be able to continue the same lifestyle. He did not want his wife to move into an apartment due to the sudden loss of his $35,000 a year in income. He figured that if they had two children over the next five years, the money from the life insurance would cover the family expenses until all their children graduated from high school. La Toya was making $45,000 a year, and she also needed 25 years of life insurance coverage. $45,000 x 25 equaled $1,125,000 that Marcus would need to raise the children at their same standard of living. Marcus would need to pay someone to take the children to practice, help them with their school-work and watch them during the summer if some-thing happened to La Toya. Marcus's monthly term life insurance cost only $45 a month, and La Toya's costs $50 a month. Marcus and La Toya felt a sense of relief because they had made the first significant step in their lives to build generational wealth. Most families never get back to normal after the sudden loss of a spouse. The most com-mon reason is that the family does not have life insurance, or their employer's life insurance policy is only two times the employee's annual salary at most which leave them begging for money to cover the funeral and future living costs for the children. The family will eventually have to sell their house to pay for the funeral, the spouse's auto loan, and the monthly bills. The kids suffer because they go from a life of plenty to a life of have-nots.

# Chapter Seven

# STEP 2 – FREE 401K MONEY

La Toya was already contributing to her 401K plan, but she let her employer select the investment plan for her. This was a HUGE mistake. La Toya had finished reading Build Generational Wealth on the plane ride back. She realized that she was losing out on about $300,000 for her retirement. She was invested in a target-date retirement fund, which was better than nothing, but it did not have the same rate of return as the **S&P 500**. The S&P 500 was composed of the largest performing U.S. companies (**Apple, Microsoft, Amazon, Tesla, Walmart, Home Depot, Visa, Exxon, Coca-Cola** etc.). It was like you picking the U.S. Olympic Basketball team to compete against the rest of the world. If the U.S. Olympic Basketball team (Jordan, James, Curry, etc.) played 12 games a year and lost one game, would you choose a different team to win the gold medal? Her target-date retirement fund was estimated to yield an annual yearly return of 6%.

In comparison, the S&P 500 was expected to generate an annual return of at least 9%. This 3% difference amounted to her having $300,000 less in her retirement account after 20 years of working and putting money into her retirement account. She made the change and was on her way to having a millionaire retirement. Go to www. madillard.com to see the estimated difference in an account earning a 3%, 6%, or 9% annual rate of return.

Marcus did not contribute to his 401k at work because he planned to retire on the pension that he would receive from the State of Tennessee when it was time for him to retire. Marcus had not been contributing to the State of Tennessee's 401K like the book advised him to. When Marcus realized that he was losing out on $1,750 of **FREE** money that he was eligible to add to his retirement account, Marcus felt like he was letting money fly out of the window. For every dollar up to 5% of his income that he put into his 401k account, his employer also put that same amount into his 401k account. 5% of his yearly salary was $1,750. Marcus did the calculation and realized that his employer's match of $1,750 a year going into his 401k account with an annual return of 9% over 28 years would equate to $230,000 of free money being left on the table and dumped into the trash can. Say, What! That is too much money to be thrown in the trash can. He was afraid to invest his money in the stock market because of the horror stories he heard on social media about people losing money after a major stock crash. But realizing that he was getting a 100% return on his money because his employer matched what he contributed in his 401k, Marcus realized that he was losing out on $460,000 being available for his retirement. He contacted the HR office, and within 15 minutes, they walked him through opening his 401k account. Marcus allocated 50% to Large U.S. companies, which was the same as the S&P 500, and 50% to Small U.S. companies. Marcus was pumped because he had calculated how much money he would have after investing 5% of his money in his 401k account. His employer also matched his contributions up to 5%. Each year on his birthday, Marcus rebalanced his 401K balance back to 50% Large U.S. companies and 50% Small U.S. companies so that he was not too overweighted when Large U.S. companies went way up or way down and vice versa for small U.S. companies.

# Chapter Eight

## STEP 3 – PAY OFF THE CREDIT CARD AND CONSUMER LOANS

L a Toya had taken out a $10,000 consumer loan to pay for the wedding decorations, pictures, etc. She owed $35,000 in student loans, $18,000 for her auto loan, and $6,000 on her credit cards. Marcus did not have a student loan since his father and Uncle paid for his college tuition. He lived with his parents throughout college, but he owed $30,000 on his truck and $7,500 on his credit cards. Since Marcus moved into La Toya's apartment, there would be some cost savings at the end of the month from Marcus not having to pay a monthly rent, water, cable, and electric payment plus their combined auto insurance bill. Still, they needed to crunch the numbers to see just how much of a saving it would be. The total combined savings at the end of the month totaled $2,000.

28

# Chapter Nine

# THE COOKOUT

C hris and Karen invited Marcus and La Toya over to their house for a cookout the following weekend. When Marcus and La Toya walked into the house, everyone congratulated them. Chris and Karen had a lovely home. They had installed a pool in the backyard two years ago, and they had just remodeled the kitchen. The house was truly marvelous. Karen was celebrating her birthday and was feeling quite excited about life. She went to the dealership and leased a convertible luxury car for three years that morning. Chris and Karen lived the good life; they lived life to the fullest and spared no expense. Chris needed to run to the store to buy some more ice, so Marcus agreed to ride to the store with him. Chris's truck was a beast. It had a Hemi engine, heated and cooled leather seats, chrome rims, and high-end speakers. Chris was in year 3 of his 7-year $55,000 car loan. Marcus tried talking to Chris about putting money into his 401K, but Chris did not want to talk about saving money for the future. He was too busy enjoying life today!

As Chris and Marcus returned to the house, Renae was pulling up. Karen was excited to see everyone again. Karen asked La Toya when they would buy a home as Renae walked into the kitchen. La Toya said they would buy a house once they paid off their consumer loans, credit cards, and auto loans. Renae asked why they were going to wait since they only had one rent payment etc., and they could combine their income together for a house payment. La Toya explained that they wanted to build generational wealth. The sooner they paid off their consumer loans, the sooner they could build long-lasting wealth. This caught Renae's attention. The burgers were done, and everyone started listening to the great experiences that Marcus and La Toya had in South Africa.

When Marcus and La Toya returned home, they reviewed their bills and income to determine how much money would be available at the end of the month, which totaled $2,000. They decided to take the $2,000 in extra cash and pay off La Toya's credit card, then Marcus's credit card. Seven months later, they had La Toya's and Marcus's credit cards paid off; next on the list was La Toya's consumer loan, then La Toya's Auto Loan, and finally Marcus's truck loan. After a bill was paid off in full, they added that back into the extra $2,000 a month they were already using to pay off their other bills. At first, La Toya was paying the bare minimum on her credit card, which was $240 a month. At that rate, it would take her 14 years to pay her credit card off and a whopping $11,775 in total payments. The jewelry, clothes, and shoes that she purchased using her credit card would cost her double the original price that she paid.

La Toya invited Renae to come over after that Sunday's church service to finish catching up. After talking about how outstanding the church service was, Renae asked La Toya again, " Why are you and Marcus still living in an apartment. La Toya explained that they were building generational wealth, which begins with having easy-to-follow wealth-building principles. First, buy life insurance to protect your family from going bankrupt; second, invest in your TSP or 401K account to take advantage of the 100% FREE money match that their employer offers; third, pay off consumer debt; fourth, invest in an Individual Retirement Account (IRA) and; fifth, put money into a custodial or child savings account. If you want to buy a house, you can buy the home after paying off all consumer debt, even if you are not putting money into your IRA. Renae was intrigued by what she was learning. She was single and did not have a lot of debt. Renae went to Nashville State Community College for two years so that she did not have to take out any student loans for her first two years of college. She did take out a consumer loan to fully furnish her apartment and go on a long vacation the year after she graduated from Middle Tennessee State University. She owed $8,000 on her consumer loan and $15,000 on her auto loan. She was already contributing to her 401K and was 100% invested in the large company index fund. She rebalanced her account to 50% Large U.S. companies and 50% Small U.S. companies. Renae decided to cut back on some of her extracurricular activities. As a result, she quickly saved $1,000 to put into her savings account to cover a broken washing machine, a water heater leak, a flat tire, or a $500 auto deductible. She was on fire to pay off her consumer loan and car payment. Since she did not have any children, she wondered if it was worth buying life insurance. La Toya explained to her that it is cheaper to purchase life insurance when you are younger. The older you get, the more expensive it becomes each year. Renae thought about it and figured that it was better to buy a 25-year term life insurance for $500,000 which would cost her $30 a month. This would suffice for now unless she got married or adopted a child.

# Chapter Ten

# BUILD GENERATIONAL WEALTH WITH LIFE INSURANCE

It was Thanksgiving, and Marcus and La Toya decided to eat dinner at Uncle Walter's house. Marcus and La Toya thanked Uncle Walter and his wife Karen for paying for their honeymoon trip. Karen explained that a church couple had gifted them the book "Build Generational Wealth," It changed their lives. It had changed their lives so much that Uncle Walter and Aunt Karen retired 8 years ago while all their friends were still working.

Marcus and La Toya could not believe what they were hearing. So, you mean you retired when you were around 57? You got that right. I thought that you all did not have enough money and could not afford things.

Uncle Walter and Aunt Karen smiled and laughed. We can afford to buy a nice car and live in a big house, but we would like to leave some assets to our children instead of leaving them with mountains of debt. Aunt Karen told them that she received $500,000 from her parents' life insurance when they passed away. This is why we could afford to pay for Marcus's tuition. We prefer to invest in education so that the future generation can build generational wealth. This all made sense to Marcus and LaToya. Uncle Walter and Aunt Karen told Marcus and La Toya they wanted to invest in Marcus' college education. They knew deep down that his college education would allow him to make $800,000 more in lifetime earnings which would benefit the next generation. Marcus and La Toya were perplexed and had no idea what Uncle Walter and Aunt Karen were talking about. Uncle Walter and Aunt Karen created an educational trust fund to help pay the college expenses of other family members. They said that they put

$500,000 in the account to get the educational trust fund started and, in return, will ask each family to put $50 a month into the account when their child starts first grade. When the child starts college, the fund will contribute up to $20,000 a year towards their college expenses. Marcus and La Toya were astonished by what they had just heard. They said that it was a fantastic idea. They called for a family meeting at Christmas to go over how the educational trust fund would be managed and how the college payments would be made. All the family members agreed, and everyone made their first contribution to the educational trust fund.

# Chapter Eleven

## NEW YEAR CELEBRATION

Marcus and LaToya brought in the New Year at church. They were thankful for having the financial discipline to pay off their credit cards. Meanwhile, Chris and Karen decided to go to Paris to celebrate the New Year in style. They posted pictures of the Eifel Tower, the Paris skyline, and their gourmet meals online. From the looks of it, they were having a wonderful time.

Juan called Marcus to wish him a Happy New Year and asked him if they had traveled somewhere special. Marcus responded and said that they could not afford to. Juan was perplexed because he knew that Marcus and LaToya were making good money. So, Juan asked Marcus what they were doing with their money. Marcus explained to Juan that he was implementing the 5 steps to building generational wealth. Juan and Lisa had just spent $2,000 on tickets and a hotel room to travel to Spain to celebrate the New Year. Juan wanted to build generational wealth, so he ordered the book as soon as he got off the phone with Marcus. Juan and Lisa made drastic changes as soon as the book arrived. Since Juan was in the U.S. Army, he stayed on base and did not have to pay as much as others did for housing and gasoline. This allowed Juan and Lisa to splurge on other things. Lisa had just started working at the Post Exchange in the HR department making $30,000 a year. However, Juan and Lisa were not making as much money as most married couples earned since Lisa always had to find a new job every time Juan was assigned to a different military base. Juan and Lisa did not have student loans because Juan joined the U.S. Army a year after graduating from high school. Juan put 5% of his salary into his Thrift Savings plan, but it was in the F fund earning him only 1% a year. Juan changed his future payroll allocation to 50% in the C Fund (Large U.S. companies) and 50% in the S fund (Small U.S. companies). Likewise, he rebalanced the money in his TSP to 50% C fund and 50% S fund.

# Chapter Twelve

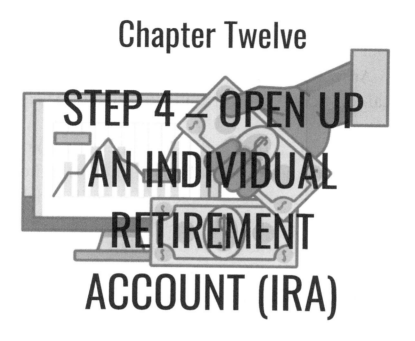

# STEP 4 – OPEN UP AN INDIVIDUAL RETIREMENT ACCOUNT (IRA)

J uan and Lisa also opened an IRA account with Vanguard since they had the lowest fees. They put $500 into a Roth IRA account for Juan, and they put $500 per month into a Roth IRA account for Lisa. Instead of paying a 5% commission every time they purchased stock plus the fund's administration fee, they only had to pay a .03% vanguard administration fee. Instead of only $950 going into their Roth IRAs, the entire $1,000 was invested in their ROTH IRA account minus the small .03% administration fee. Juan was approaching 20 years of service in the U.S. Army, so he started to think about his retirement options. After 20 years in the U.S. Army, he decided to retire and get a job in the local community or work until he reached 25 years of service.

Marcus and La Toya had paid off their auto loans and were ready to buy a house. They searched for the perfect place and a family-friendly neighborhood. Since they just had a baby girl named Stephanie, they knew they wanted to find a home close to an excellent elementary school. They searched and searched but could not find a stylish and modern house like Chris and Karen lived in. They settled for a smaller home but in an excellent school district in another subdivision. The housing prices were just too high in that subdivision. They signed up for a 20-year mortgage since they only had LaToya's student loan left to pay off.

Marcus really enjoyed having conversations with his uncle Walter. Marcus and La Toya were ready to open their IRA accounts, so Marcus met with his Uncle Walter to get advice from him. His uncle told him that he had received $20,000 in annual dividend payments from his IRA. Marcus wanted to know more. Uncle Walter explained to Marcus that he invests in dividend growth stocks for his individual retirement account from the stocks classified as dividend aristocrats. Dividend aristocrats are U.S. companies that have paid a dividend for the last 25 years. Uncle Walter considered these companies to be the best of the best because these companies had weathered every financial storm that came their way. Yet, they continued to pay a dividend to their shareholders.

Uncle water thought this was a guaranteed way to receive a 2% to 3% return on his investments each year. Uncle Walter started investing in dividend-paying stocks after reading an article that said Warren Buffett gets about $672 million in dividend income per year from the Coca-Cola stock he purchased over twenty years ago. The article really fascinated Uncle Walter because he could not believe how much of an impact a yearly dividend growth increase of 8% to 10% per year plus an annual dividend yield of around 2% to 4% could have such a massive impact on your wealth twenty years later. The article highlighted that Warren Buffett was receiving yearly dividends worth more than his original purchase price of the Coca-Cola stock; this was fascinating. Uncle Walter realized that he was receiving the annual price appreciation for the value of his stocks, plus he was also receiving a guaranteed dividend from these stocks, which provided him with a huge safety net for his retirement.

Uncle Walter told Marcus that he must do his own research because everyone's risk tolerance is different. Once he buys a dividend aristocrat stock, he never sells it unless the company cuts its dividend. Other than that, he plans to never sell the stock, no matter if the stock goes up and down in selling price. If someone knocked on your door and offered you $300,000 for your house that you paid $400,000 for, would you sell it? Then the next day, someone else came to your door and offered you $250,000 for your house. Would you sell it? This is what is happening in the stock market, one day, the price to buy or sell will be high, and a few months later, it will be lower. Uncle Walter told Marcus that he liked to buy the dividend aristocrat stocks when a big news story said that the stock prices were down more than 20%. Uncle Walter saw the stock decline as a special promotional sale. Marcus liked how Uncle Walter explained this to him; it was like going to the jewelry store and eyeing a diamond necklace that usually costs

$1,000 but was on sale for $950. He said people would be willing to pay $950 for something selling for $1,000 a few days ago. This is the same thing that is happening with stocks. The price of a stock will go up and down, but if you look at the stock's price increase over a 10- and 20-year period, you will see a steady rise in its value.

Uncle water also explained that Marcus must choose an investment style that he was comfortable with and stick to it. He emphasized that some investment styles work better during certain economic times. The worst thing that Marcus could do would be to change his investment style when his account balance went down. It is usual for stocks to go up and down, but over a 10-year time horizon, the pattern should show an upward increase in value. His investment period should be for a minimum of 10 years before he sells a stock unless the stock fails to meet his pre-established criteria.

In Uncle Walter's case, he only had one stock selling rule that he lived by; if a company no longer paid a dividend, he would sell it because it did not meet his investment philosophy. He only wanted to buy stocks that survived all types of financial markets and were still able to pay a dividend for at least 25 years. Excited about what he was hearing, Marcus opened an IRA account for himself and La Toya. He searched for stocks that paid a dividend for more than 25 years in the United States of America. He found ten stocks he liked, so he set up his account to take out $250 every two weeks to purchase them. So, every two weeks, he bought $25 worth of stock for each of the ten companies for $250. He did the same thing for La Toya's IRA. After three months went by, Marcus and La Toya started receiving dividend payments from each of their ten stocks. Marcus was ecstatic every time he received a notification about a recent dividend payment going into his account. Marcus knew that his $0.02 dividend payments one day and $0.04 another day would increase and increase over the years. He took his dividend payments and bought more stock with it. Marcus's goal was to receive $15,000 in dividend payments from their individual retirement accounts.

# Chapter Thirteen

# BUYING A HOME CAN BUILD WEALTH

As luck would have it, Juan and Lisa got transferred to Fort Campbell, Kentucky, just in time to make it to Marcus and La Toya's housewarming party in Murfreesboro, TN, which was 1 and a half hours away. Chris and Karen pulled up in Chris's newly purchased Titanium edition 4x4 black pickup truck. It had a big touch screen on the front dashboard, TV screens in the back, tan leather seats, and shiny alloy rims. Marcus and LaToya were still driving their same old cars. Renae was happy to see everyone back in the same room together. Renae brought the happy couple a gift card to the hardware store. The happy couple, Chris and Karen, brought them a charcoal grill and a large outdoor potted plant. Juan and Lisa brought them an expresso coffee machine to keep them energized. They were having fun, chatting about life. Chris and Karen were planning their next vacation as usual. This time they were going to the Bahamas. Juan was thinking about life after the U.S. Army because it was becoming more and more difficult for Lisa to find a job after every move. They were ready to settle down in one place so that Lisa could have her forever job. Although Juan and Lisa stayed on the military base, they were prepared to buy a home.

Renae kept thinking about how much she was paying for rent and began thinking more and more about what she read in the book. She realized that she would not be able to create generational wealth if she did not own her home. If Renae continued to pay $700 a month for 25 years, it would total $210,000 of rent payments but would be worth $0 to her when she moved out of the apartment and returned the key. Since she was single, she did not have the luxury of paying the mortgage with a spouse. After Renae paid off her consumer and auto loans, she looked for a town-house in a subdivision that did not have a lot of commuter traffic. She wanted to make sure that the area offered a little more privacy than the other houses that she had been seeing. She secured a mortgage loan and put down 10% on a $200,000 townhouse. She signed up for a twenty-year mortgage since she wanted to invest some money in an Individual Retirement Account and needed to buy new appliances for the house.

A few months later, Juan and Lisa found a place in Clarksville, Tennessee, right off Need-more road. They chose a 30-year mortgage because Lisa had not found a job when they returned to the U.S. after working in Frankfurt, Germany. Juan used his VA Loan and put down 5% on the house. Once Lisa started working again, they planned to pay extra towards the mortgage to have the house paid off in 20 years. At their housewarming party, they were so thankful for the gardening tools that everyone gave them. They would have to cut the yard themselves for the first time after years of the U.S. Government cutting the grass on the base. Marcus and La Toya just had a baby boy named Scott a few months ago, so he

was the center of attention at the housewarming
party.

# Chapter Fourteen

# UNEMPLOYED

Chris refused to put money into a 401K account. Lisa was still putting money into her 401K account, but she did not see the need to put money into an IRA account. Chris pulled up at work in typical fashion and scrolled into the office, but this morning something was a little different in the office. His boss was sitting in the conference room with five executives he had never seen before. There had always been rumors of the company being bought out, but nothing ever happened. Chris went to lunch, and when he returned to the office, he was told that the company had been sold. Management informed Chris that they would transfer the operations from Tennessee to Texas. Chris asked what would happen to his position, and he was told that it was no longer needed and that he would be given a generous 2-month severance package. Chris was furious because he and Karen had just refinanced their mortgage for 30 more years so that they could take $40,000 of equity out of the house to pay off their credit cards, buy a boat and build a new garage for it in their backyard to protect it from the snow in the winter. Chris packed up his belongings in the office and headed home to tell Karen the devastating news.

The HR manager handed Chris an envelope that explained his severance package, but he was too upset at the time to open it up. When Chris pulled into the driveway, his son Jack was outside playing basketball with the neighborhood friends. Meanwhile, his daughter was having a pool party with some of her friends. He greeted everyone and then went upstairs to digest what had just happened. Karen arrived home 20 minutes later and found Chris visibly upset. Chris handed Karen the brown envelope to open. Karen saw a severance package on the front of the envelope. She immediately started to tear up and cry. Oh, no, what are we going to do, Chris? Karen said. How are we going to pay for everything? I do not know, Chris said to Karen. The severance package was for two months' salary plus HR assistance with a career counseling agency.

Two months later, Chris's truck was reposed. He tried to sell it just before they came to reprocess his truck, but Chris could not find anyone willing to pay $45,000 for his Titanium edition truck which was the loan amount owed to the bank. He could not believe that no one was willing to pay $45,000 for it. Even if he sold it for $35,000, he would still owe the bank $10,000, which was the only offer that he received. After Chris's car got reposed, Chris and Karen were finally ready to make a financial change. They sold off everything that they could. Marcus got rid of his boat, and Karen sold off her dresses and shoes, but that was not enough. They put their house up for sale and hoped for a quick sale.

Meanwhile, they started looking for a place to live that was within their budget, but it was difficult with their credit card balance going back up, the other loans, and Karen's auto lease. Ten days after putting the house up for sale, they found a buyer. Now they had a decision to make, where would they live next. They decided to rent a three-bedroom apartment and put their stuff in storage.

# Chapter Fifteen

# TRAGEDY HITS —NO LIFE INSURANCE FOR THEIR CHILD

I t was a typical Friday night, and Renae watched her ten-year-old niece while her sister went to a concert with her husband. Renae was having a blast with her niece. They had painted each other's nails and were sitting down watching a Disney movie when her cell phone rang. Her sister and brother-in-law were hit by a drunk driver and passed away. She had agreed to watch her niece that night, not knowing that her parents would never return. It was terrible timing for the family because her sister and brother-in-law only had their employer's life insurance worth one year of their combined annual salary of $40,000 in total. Her sister had just switched employers, and her brother-in-law worked in construction. Seeing how things turned out for her sister Cindy, Renae called up her life insurance agent and had her niece listed as her beneficiary for the $500,000 life insurance policy she signed up for years ago.

When Chris and Karen sold their house, they received $20,000 after paying their real estate agent and other miscellaneous costs. They used the $20,000 in equity from selling their home to put in the bank until Chris found a job. Hearing about Renae's niece, they immediately bought 20 years of term life insurance since their children were 8 and twelve years away from graduation. Chris read the book Accidental Success – Accidental Millionaire Retirement by Michael Dillard and was inspired by how the author was unemployed, knocked on doors until he found a job, and then accidentally became a U.S. Diplomat. Chris decided to take a job as a customer service representative that was paying way less than he earned at his last job, but this time he knew that it was not about how much he made but about how much he saved. Later, they took the $20,000 in the bank and bought a mid-size SUV for $15,000 in cash so that he could drive to work. This time Chris signed up for his employer's 401K plan and contributed 5% to get the company match. Chris and Lisa were following the 5-step plan. Next, they began paying an extra $600 per month to pay off their bills.

# Chapter Sixteen

# JUAN RETIRES FROM THE U.S. ARMY

Juan decided to retire from the U.S. Army after twenty years of service. For all his arduous work and sacrifices, he received a $20,000 a year government pension worth $500,000. Juan came up with this calculation by taking $20,000 and dividing it by 4%, equalling $500,000. This is how much money Juan would have had to save up on his own to withdraw 4% per year. 4% is considered the industry standard safe withdrawal rate without running out of money years into your retirement.

Juan retired and became a real estate agent in the local area. He was able to keep his affordable health care insurance after retiring from the military, which made it easier for him to work for himself as a real estate agent. Lisa had been working for a local real estate agency for the last several years, which is why Juan wanted to become a real estate agent. Lisa was so excited to have a job and not worry about searching for a new job every three to five years. With Juan's guaranteed $20,000 a year pension, they figured that they could save enough money in their IRA accounts and retire with enough of a safety net once their mortgage was paid off.

The transmission on Lisa's car went out, so Juan and Lisa looked for a vehicle while remembering what they had read about not having a car payment for years. They wanted to pay cash so that they could focus on building generational wealth. They went from car lot to car lot looking for a vehicle that had less than 36,000 miles and was in good condition. They got excited because they had found a mid-size SUV in their price range of $20,000; however, when they test drove it, the car was making a weird noise. This started to make Juan and Lisa worried. They said that if they had a brand-new car, they would not have to worry about car troubles for at least the next five years, but a new car would cost $40,000. Juan did the math and told Lisa that they could buy two cars for the price of 1. So, if we purchased a $20,000 car and it lasted us for three to five years, and then we bought another $20,000 car, and if that car also lasted 3-5 years, then we would be in the same or a better situation. Lisa got the point that Juan was making. They could spend $20,000 today on a car; when the car had a problem, they could fix it and spend another $3,000, and if something else happened to the car, they would have to pay another $4,000, but the total amount of money spent on the vehicle over a five-year time period would be about $27,000 which would be cheaper than paying $40,000 for a brand-new car because of the 5-year warranty that is included.

Lisa looked online, and she saw a nice shiny car that was just what she was looking for at CarMax. It was marked below Kelley Blue Book value, so Juan and Lisa hurried out the door to look at it. When Juan and Lisa walked up to CarMax and into the store, they met Bill. Bill had been working for CarMax for the last 10 years. He asked them what they were looking for, and Juan explained that they were looking for a mid-size SUV for around $20,000. Bob said that it would be tough to find a mid-size SUV for $20,000 big enough for his family. However, Bob did not know that Juan and Lisa had been researching buying a car for the last three weeks, so they knew what options were available.

Juan asked to go look outside to see what was on the lot. Bob pointed in the direction of the SUVs on the car lot. Lisa walked along the car lot and right up to the car that she saw online. Lisa opened the car door to the mid-size SUV and was relieved that it did not smell, the interior was in excellent condition, and the engine looked nice and clean. Juan walked back into the lobby and told Bob that they wanted to test drive the vehicle. Bob took their driver's license, made a copy, and then handed them the keys. Juan drove the car along the highway, and then he pulled over so that Lisa could test the vehicle. Lisa was overly impressed with the car. However, it was 6 years old and just a little older than what they really wanted, but it was a Toyota Highlander with only 60,000 miles. Juan and Lisa had researched how long a typical Toyota vehicle lasts. A Toyota SUV can easily last up to 250,000 miles from their research. Sold!

---

Renae's niece was doing well in school, but Renae wanted to keep her busy during the summer, so Renae purchased an online educational software program called IXL. The software showed Renae what her niece was good at and what subjects she struggled with. She liked IXL because she could track the number of hours her niece was active online. Renae's niece asked her for an allowance, so Renae agreed that if she completed 45 minutes of IXL Monday through Friday and 2 hours on Saturday and Sunday, she could have an allowance of $20 per week. Her niece was excited because she could buy those brand-new tennis shoes that she had been eyeing at the shoe store. Renae really wanted her niece to get a scholarship for college instead of starting her life with student loan debt.

La Toya and Marcus had been living in their new house for 5 years. It was that time of the year to receive their annual tax notification letter in the mail. Usually, they would toss the mail to the side since their taxes were included in their mortgage payment. To their surprise, when the tax letter arrived, their house had gone up in value more than they had expected. Since they lived in a very sought-after community because of the middle school and high school in their neighborhood, their house had gone up 7% per year, which was way above the U.S. annual average of 3%. Their home had gone up by $75,000. Marcus and La Toya were thrilled to see this because they could see first-hand how they built generational wealth for their children.

# Chapter Seventeen

# STEP 5 – OPEN UP A CUSTODIAL ACCOUNT

M arcus got a promotion at his job, which he was overly excited about. Marcus's annual salary was going to increase by $5,000 per year. Marcus and La Toya decided to put $2,500 from his salary increase towards their mortgage and $2,500 in the custodial accounts for their children.

When it comes to creating generational wealth, the final piece is that you must set aside a savings account for your children. Your children need to learn that it is normal to save money for the future at an early age. The most important thing that a parent can teach their children is the habit of keeping some of their money earned today for tomorrow's sorrow. Do not let your children get in the habit of getting $20 and spending $20 as soon as they receive it. This creates a mindset of Now, Now, Now, and not thinking about what sorrows will come tomorrow. Thus, you need to open an investment account for your child based on your tax situation, your income, and your long-term goals for them.

You can open a child savings account, a prepaid tuition account, a 529 plan, or whatever investment vehicle that you like, but the most important thing is that you open at least one of these accounts. The goal is to teach your children how to spend money, invest money, and manage money at an early age. When a child is 5 years old, tomorrow seems like forever, but when they turn 13, they start to grasp how far off tomorrow is compared to next week. Teach your child the concept of how a dollar invested today in the S&P 500 will grow slow and steady over time. Marcus and La Toya opened custodial accounts for each of their children when they were born with the plan of taking money out when they were about to graduate from high school to buy them a car. As their children got older, they explained what the S&P 500 was and allowed them to select stocks from the list of dividend aristocrats stocks each year on their birthday. Make investing for the future a regular part of your children's everyday lives so that it becomes a normal part of life.

# Chapter Eighteen

# PUTTING IT ALL TOGETHER

After Chris and Karen had paid off all their consumer debt, Chris was ready to repurchase a house. Karen was afraid that if they bought another house, Chris would want to buy another boat, which would require a bigger truck to pull the boat. She also thought that Chris would want to trade in his current truck for another one. Karen kept telling Chris that they were not ready to buy a new house. Chris told Karen that things were different this time because Lisa's car was paid off, and his vehicle was paid off, plus they no longer pay for vacations using credit cards. In addition, Chris had been investing money into his 401K account, which meant that he finally had money built up in a retirement account. Chris and Karen recently opened an IRA account with Vanguard to put money into it since there was a tax benefit that they could take advantage of. Chris wanted to retire on his own terms instead of a company forcing him to retire, so he was very eager to live below his financial means. When Chris showed Karen the financial numbers, Karen said yes, the numbers looked good, and they could start looking for a house in six months. Chris was delighted that Karen had agreed to buy another home. This time Chris started looking for places they could afford even if one of them became unexpectedly unemployed for six months.

Since Chris and Karen's oldest child was in college and their second child was in high school, they wanted to live in an area where the high school had plenty of after-school activities. Chris and Karen found a very affordable house that was well within their budget, so they decided to buy it. The realtor insisted that Chris and Karen could afford to buy a home that was twice the price of the house they were looking for. The realtor kept showing Chris some great places that had just been built, but Chris and Karen did not want to repeat the same thing that happened to them the last time when he lost his job. Yes, those other homes were spectacular with their nicely manicured lawn and big porch, but they also came with huge mortgages, which Chris and Karen were not interested in.

Shortly after that, Chris and Karen moved into their forever home and invited Marcus and La-Toya, Juan and Lisa, and Renae to look at their new place. At the housewarming party, Chris and Karen called for a toast. They each thanked Marcus and La Toya for making them read the book Build Generational Wealth. They said that the book changed their lives and wished that they had read the book before they got married and started taking on tons of debt. They said they had wasted so much money on vacations and things that did not increase in value. They thought about how much they could have saved in their retirement accounts if they had not taken all those fancy vacations and did not lease all those fancy cars.

# Chapter Nineteen

# $50,000 SCHOLARSHIP FOR COLLEGE

Time had passed, and La Toya and Marcus's oldest child was in the 9th grade. She had just received all A's on her first report card and thought it would be a suitable time to ask her parents if she could work at the fast-food chain down the street. Marcus and La Toya kept emphasizing the importance of a high GPA. They said that at this point in life, her job was to make straight A's so that she could receive a $30,000 to $50,000 college scholarship, which would be more than what she would earn working at the local fast-food chain for three years. Marcus and La Toya made sure that at 6:00 pm, their children sat down at the dining table and did their homework, read, or did online learning using IXL.

Marcus always thought to himself, what if his parents had emphasized the importance of studying and having a high GPA during high school? How much would that have helped him with his career choice? Marcus struggled to find a high-paying job after he graduated from college because he did not do an internship while he was in college. He kept thinking that he could have been a doctor or dentist if he had taken his grades more seriously. He knew that he could have been a straight-A student with an extra push from his mom or dad.

Marcus and La Toya's daughter, Stephanie, graduated from high school with straight A's and was offered a scholarship to attend Vanderbilt University. The $50,000 yearly scholarship came with free room and board. All the sacrifices that Stephanie made to study instead of hanging out and relaxing at home had paid off more than she could have ever imagined. Cheers to no college debt! Marcus and La Toya were so happy that they emphasized the importance of studying and making A's. They were building generational knowledge and generational wealth. Their second child, Scott, was making straight A's as well and was looking forward to receiving a scholarship so that he, too, could graduate from college debt-free. After their oldest daughter completed her first year of college, she completed an internship at a local law firm. Marcus was so happy for her because Stephanie did not repeat the same mistake he made by working at a fast-food company for quick money instead of gaining valuable work experience. He focused on making money to buy clothes and eat out during the summer instead of gaining office experience.

Their oldest daughter was offered a job at a local law firm after she graduated with a four-year degree, but she turned it down because she wanted to go back to Graduate School to get her law degree. She applied to Vanderbilt law school and got accepted. Instead of living in an apartment, she decided to live with her parents since most of her time would be spent studying all day and night.

After graduating from law school, their daughter received a $120,000 job offer with special incentives. She just needed to pass the bar exam, and she would be making the same amount of money that both her parents earned together. This was great news, the family tradition of sitting down at 6:00 pm to study so that in the future, they would have a fantastic career for the rest of their life had become a reality. After passing the bar exam, Stephanie decided to wait a year before moving out of her parents' house. She wanted to save up money for a down payment on a house in a great school district to continue the journey of building generational wealth by owning a home. She could easily afford to move into an apartment and pay $800 a month if she wanted. She already knew what would happen if she immediately moved out of her parent's home and into an apartment. After four years of living in the apartment and saving up for a down payment, the apartment complex would tell her, "Thanks for staying. Please come back again." Her $800 a month rent payment x 12 months x 4 years would total $38,400 in non-refundable rent. After four years of living in her house, she would have gained $30,000 to $40,000 of equity in her home. So, if she sold her house, she would receive a check of $30,000 to $40,000 minus any real estate sales cost. It was an easy decision for her to sacrifice 1 year of her life living with her parents to build generational wealth early in life.

As soon as Scott graduated from medical school at Meharry Medical College, Marcus and La Toya started thinking about retiring. They crunched the numbers, and it showed that based upon the $150,000 in Marcus's 401K account and the $450,000 in La Toya's 401K account, they had a total of $600,000 in their 401K's. If they withdraw 4% of the balance that is in their 401k (4% safe withdrawal rule), then they would be able to safely withdraw $24,000 in annual income in year one. If their 401k balance increased the next year to $618,000 they would withdraw $24,720 ($618,000 x 4%). Since Marcus worked for the State of Tennessee, he was eligible to receive a yearly pension of $12,000. They had accumulated $400,000 in Marcus's IRA account because some of his dividend aristocrat stocks had performed well and $400,000 in La Toya's IRA account. In total, they had accumulated over $800,000 in their IRA accounts. Using the 4% rule they could safely withdraw $32,000 ($800,000 x 4%). So now they were looking at $68,000 in annual income, which did not include the amount they would receive from Social Security. They decided that the $68,000 a year plus an estimate of $32,000 in social security payments for a combined total of $100,000 would be enough to let them enjoy a pleasant retirement.

# Chapter Twenty

# CONCLUSION

In life, I have learned that it is not about where you start, but what it is that you choose to do to stay in the race. You can choose to be upset that you are not at the front of the line when the guns go off or you can choose to do something about it by taking a single step. I am always cognizant that despite the fact that I did not come from a home with wealthy parents, things could have been worse for me. There are those that have started life off so far behind me and yet they too have chosen to run instead of sitting down. I am always inspired by the lives of those that came from nothing and made something for themselves and others.

It is true that there are those who will always have more and do more because they had a great start, but you should not let that control your life. There have been many people who came from riches or made millions, yet they ended up broke because they stopped moving. As long as you never give up and take action by at least crawling if you cannot walk, or walking if you cannot jog, you will be successful.

I hope that this book has inspired you to take some sort of action that you have been putting off for a long time. I look forward to you sharing your results with others.

*Please help a friend by taking one minute of your time to provide a review of the book online wherever you purchased the book.*

Your action will inspire others to act.

***Thanks for your support!***

*The secrets revealed in this fictional book are not actual financial advice. Please see your financial advisor, attorney, and or consult the IRS*

# Chapter Twenty-one

# Author

M ichael Dillard was born in Portsmouth, Virginia but was raised for most of his childhood in Clarksville, Tennessee. He graduated from Northeast High School and is a member of the Austin Peay State University Upward Bound Program. As a Foreign Service Officer he has worked in the Dominican Republic, Zambia, Afghanistan, the Democratic Republic of Congo, and South Africa.

In addition, he served four years in the U.S. Army as a radio repairer. He was stationed at Ft. Carson, Colorado; Camp Casey, South Korea, and Ft. Stewart, Georgia.

He received his Bachelors Degree in Interdisciplinary Studies from Middle Tennessee State University, a Master in Business Administration with a concentration in Financial Planning from Strayer University, and a Masters Degree in Accounting from Liberty University. He is a certified ICF Coach who helps leaders build motivated teams and helps people to build generational wealth. Schedule a one of kind coaching session with him today!

www.madillard.com
info@madillard.com

# Chapter Twenty-two

# Rule of 72

What is the Rule of 72?

The Rule of 72 is a calculation that estimates the number of years it takes to

double your money at a specified rate of return. If, for example, your account earns 9 percent, divide 72 by 9 to get the number of years it will take for your money to double. In this case, 8 years is what you would expect if you invested in the S&P 500.

# Rule of 72

| Years | Take 72 Divided by Average Rate of Return. This Equals Time for Your Money to Double | 100% Bond 3% | Target Date Fund 6% | 100% Stock 12% |
|---|---|---|---|---|
| 0 | | $10,000 | $10,000 | $10,000 |
| 6 | | | | $20,000 |
| 12 | | | $20,000 | $40,000 |
| 18 | | | | $80,000 |
| 24 | | $20,000 | $40,000 | $160,000 |
| 30 | | | | $320,000 |
| 36 | | | $80,000 | $640,000 |
| 42 | | | | $1,280,000 |
| 48 | | $40,000 | $160,000 | $2,560,000 |

(Bond column: "Ready to Retire?" / "Ready to Retire?")

If, for example, your account earns 12 percent when the stock market is at an all-time high, divide 72 by 12 to get the number of years it will take for your money to double. In this case, 6 years.

# Chapter Twenty-three

# S&P 500

W hat is the S&P 500?

The S&P 500 is the industry's first index fund for individual investors, the 500 Index Fund is a low-cost way to gain diversified exposure to the U.S. stock market. The fund offers exposure to **500 of the largest U.S. companies**, which span many different industries and account for about three-fourths of the U.S. stock market's value. Because the 500 Index Fund is broadly diversified within the large-capitalization market, it is available in most 401k and IRA accounts.

As of September 30, 2021, the nine largest companies on the list of S&P 500 companies accounted for 28.1% of the market capitalization of the index and were, in order of weighting, Apple, Microsoft, Alphabet, Amazon.com, Meta Platforms, Tesla, Nvidia, Berkshire Hathaway and JPMorgan Chase.[3] The components that have increased their dividends in 25 consecutive years are known as the S&P 500 Dividend Aristocrats. (Wikipedia)

The S&P 500 index can derive about 70% of their revenue in the United States.

# Chapter Twenty-four

# 401(k) - $995K in 35 years

Your 401(k) could be worth **$995,568** after 35 years. This was calculated with your current contribution of $2,000.00 per year and a current 401(k) balance of $0. Your current plan has you contributing 5% of your annual salary of $40,000 per year. Your yearly salary increases by 1% each year.

Your 401(k) total also includes an employer match of 100% of your contributions, up to 5% of your annual salary. Your current 401(k) plan has your employer contributing $2,000.00 per year if you contribute $2,000 per year. To receive your employer's maximum match of $2,000.00, you should contribute at least 5% of your annual salary to your 401(k). Without your employer's match, your ending 401(k) would be reduced to $497,784.

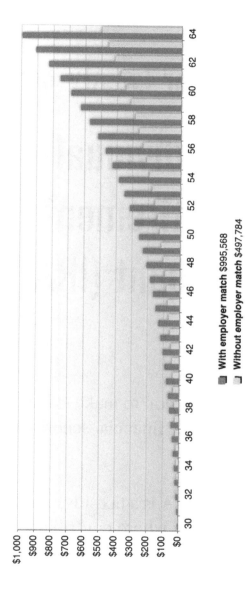

With employer match $995,568
Without employer match $497,784

# Chapter Twenty-five

# Individual Retirement Account (IRA)

W hat is an IRA?
    IRAs allow you to make tax-deferred investments to provide financial security when you retire.

Types of IRAs

- A traditional IRA is a tax-advantaged personal savings plan where contributions may be tax-deductible.

- A Roth IRA is a tax-advantaged personal savings plan where contributions are not deductible but qualified distributions may be tax-free.

If you open up an IRA account at age 35 and invest $6,000 a year until age 65, you will about $891K before taxes or $757K after taxes.

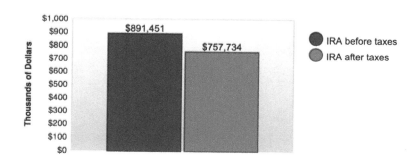

# Chapter Twenty-six

# ACCIDENTAL SUCCESS

Michael Dillard's life journey to becoming an -
**Accidental** Diplomat is a self-help guide to
achieving success in all aspects of your life.

The lessons revealed in this book will help propel you to success.

# Chapter Twenty-seven
# FREE RETIREMENT RESOURCES

Protect your family's wealth today.
Receive free information about Retirement and
Life Insurance at www.madillard.com

Made in the USA
Monee, IL
19 January 2024

51688518R00059